The Nature Kid's Guide to
BEARDED DRAGONS

DAVID ANDERSON

LP Media Inc. Publishing
Text copyright © 2026 by LP Media Inc.
All rights reserved.

For information address LP Media Inc. Publishing,
30012 Variolite St NW, Princeton MN 55371
www.lpmedia.org

Publication Data

Bearded Dragons
The Nature Kid's Guide to Bearded Dragons — First edition.

Summary: "Learn all about Bearded Dragons, the Nature Kid Way"
— Provided by publisher.

ISBN: 979-8-89818-173-4

[1. Bearded Dragons – Non-Fiction] I. Title.

Title: The Nature Kid's Guide to Bearded Dragons

CONTENTS

DESERT
DWELLERS

Crunch! A bearded dragon skitters across hot desert sand.

Bearded dragons live in dry, warm places. They call the deserts and woodlands of Australia home. These tough lizards love the heat!

Sandy ground and red rocks fill their world. A dragon may rest on a log or hide under a stone. It digs into the dirt to cool off.

Life in the desert is hard. Food and water can be tough to find. But bearded dragons are built for it.

Bearded dragons can go weeks without drinking water, getting moisture from juicy bugs and plants.

AUSSIE ANIMALS

Rustle! A bearded dragon crawls through dry Australian brush.

Australia is the only country where wild bearded dragons live. Much of the land is hot and dry. Temperatures in the outback can climb past 110°F! But bearded dragons are built for it.

Bearded dragons roam across most of the country. Some live in the red, sandy center. Others live near forests along the coast.

There are eight kinds of bearded dragons. Each kind calls a different part of the country home. The biggest can grow nearly two feet long, while the smallest, the Drysdale River bearded dragon, is only about six inches long!

SIZE CHECK

Unlike geckos and other lizards, bearded dragons cannot grow back a lost tail!

Plop! A big bearded dragon stretches long across a warm rock.

A full-grown bearded dragon is about two feet long. That is about as long as your arm! More than half of that length is tail.

These lizards weigh around one pound. They are light, but their flat, wide bodies make them look bigger, especially when they puff up to scare off a predator.

Even though they are not heavy, bearded dragons are strong climbers. In the wild, they scramble up rocks, tree stumps, and fence posts to find the best sunny spots. The higher they sit, the more important they are to other bearded dragons nearby.

BRILLIANT BEARDS

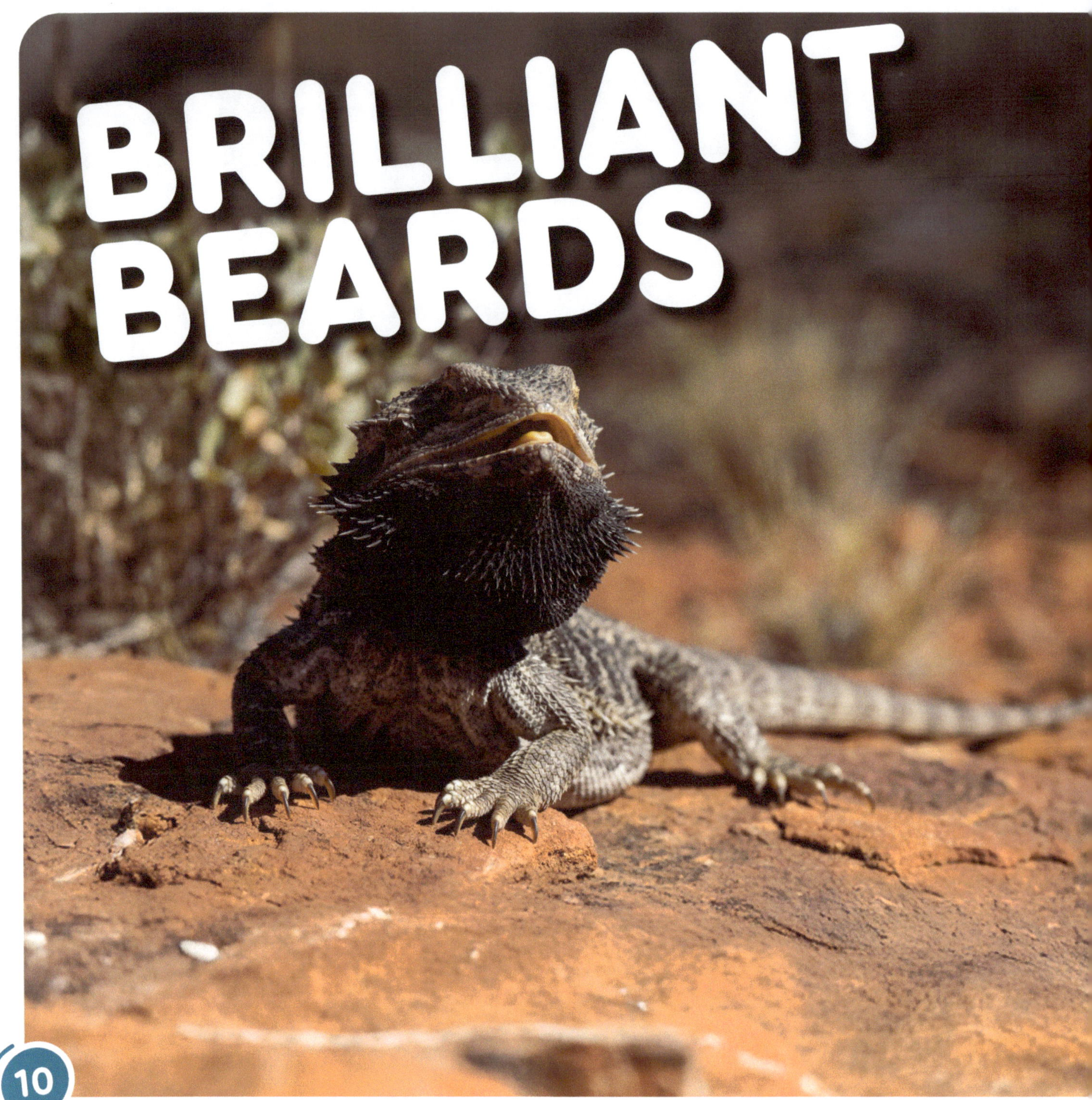

Puff! A bearded dragon flares its throat into a dark pouch.

Bearded dragons get their name from the spiny flap under their chin. When this flap puffs out, it looks like a beard! It can turn jet black.

The rest of the body is covered in small, rough scales. Four strong legs end in sharp claws. These claws help the lizard grip bark and stone.

A long, thick tail trails behind. It helps the dragon keep its balance. The whole body is built tough.

A bearded dragon's teeth don't have roots like yours do. They are fused right on top of the jawbone. If one falls out, it never grows back!

SUPER SENSES

A bearded dragon's ears are tiny holes on the sides of its head!

Flick! A bearded dragon's eye spots a cricket in the grass.

Bearded dragons have sharp eyesight. Their eyes sit on the sides of their head, which lets them see nearly all the way around themselves without turning.

A bearded dragon also has a third eye on top of its head! Look closely and you might spot a tiny dot between its other two eyes. It is called a parietal eye. It cannot see pictures like a normal eye, but it can sense light and shadow from above.

If a hawk's shadow passes overhead, this third eye helps the bearded dragon react fast, even before it looks up.

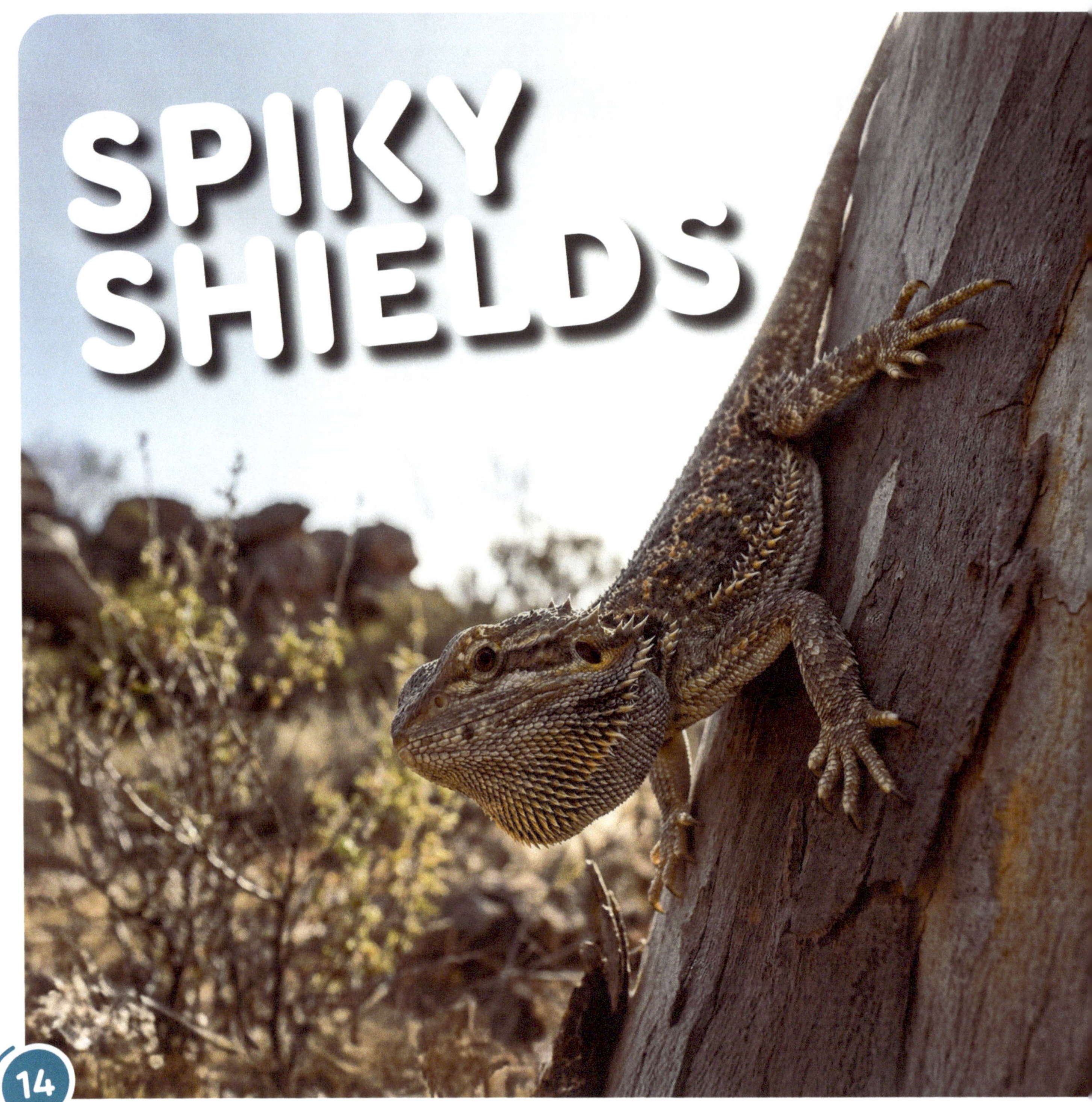

SPIKY
SHIELDS

Scritch! Sharp spines scrape along bark as a dragon climbs.

Rows of pointed spines run along a bearded dragon's body. They line the sides, the back of the head, and the throat. These spikes look sharp and mean!

But here is a surprise, the spines are actually soft and rubbery, not sharp at all. You can pet a bearded dragon without getting poked. The spines are just for show, meant to trick predators into thinking this lizard is too prickly to eat.

The spikes work like a suit of armor for the dragon.

A bearded dragon's spines are made of keratin, the same stuff as your fingernails!

BUGGY
BUFFET

Chomp! A bearded dragon bites into a bright yellow flower.

Bearded dragons eat both bugs and plants. They munch on crickets, beetles, and ants. They also gobble up worms and spiders.

Plants are part of the meal too. These lizards nibble on flowers, leaves, and soft fruit. A juicy berry is a tasty treat!

A bearded dragon is not a picky eater. It will try almost anything that fits in its mouth. This helps it survive when food is hard to find.

A bearded dragon eats more bugs as a baby and more plants as an adult!

SIT AND SNATCH

Snap! A bearded dragon snatches a beetle that wandered too close.

Bearded dragons hunt by waiting. A dragon finds a good spot and stays very still. When a bug walks by — snap! Its sticky tongue shoots out and snatches the meal in the blink of an eye.

These lizards use their sharp eyes to watch for prey. They do not chase food far. They wait for it to come close.

A bearded dragon crushes bugs with its strong jaws. It swallows its meal in big gulps. Meals do not last long for this hungry hunter!

Bearded dragons sometimes eat small lizards and even tiny mice!

DANGER
LURKS

Swoop! A bearded dragon freezes as a hawk dives from the sky.

Many animals want to eat bearded dragons. Hawks and eagles swoop down from the sky. Big snakes sneak up on them.

Goannas are large lizards that hunt bearded dragons too. Dingoes and **feral** cats may grab them. The desert is full of danger.

A bearded dragon must always stay alert. One wrong move could be its last. Keeping watch is a big part of staying alive.

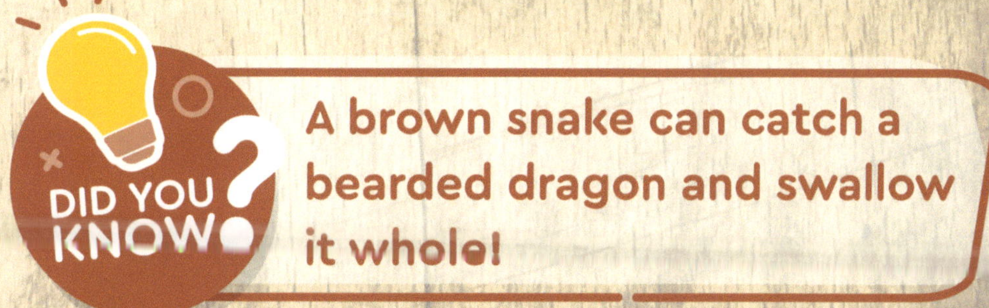

PUFF UP

Hissss! A bearded dragon puffs up wide and opens its mouth.

A bearded dragon puffs up to look as large and scary as it can. It puffs out its throat and flattens its body.

The dragon may open its mouth wide and hiss. The bright color inside can startle a predator. All of this says, 'Stay away!'

If the trick does not work, the dragon runs. It dashes to a burrow or presses flat and tries to slide under a rock.

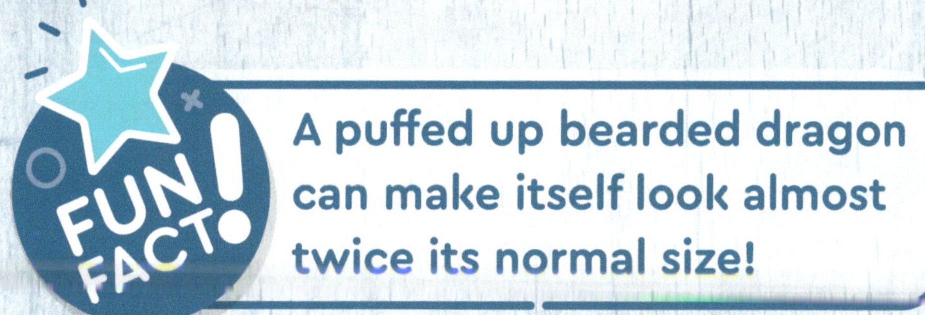

SCURRY
SCAMPER
24

Zip! A bearded dragon races across the sand on its back legs.

Bearded dragons are fast runners. When they need speed, they rise up on just their back legs! They lift their front half right off the ground and sprint on two feet, almost like a tiny dinosaur.

Scientists think running on two legs helps them go faster and breathe easier at the same time. If you ever see a bearded dragon running, watch closely, it looks like something straight out of a movie about prehistoric creatures.

A bearded dragon can sprint up to nine miles per hour – that is nearly as fast as you can run!

BASK AND
REST

Thump! A bearded dragon drops onto a flat rock to soak up the sun.

Bearded dragons are **cold-blooded**. Their bodies do not make their own heat. They need the sun to warm up each day.

Every morning, a dragon finds a sunny spot. It spreads its body wide to soak up heat. This is called **basking**.

When the day gets too hot, the dragon moves to shade. At night, it tucks under a rock or hides beneath bark to sleep.

Bearded dragons are most active in the first few hours after sunrise!

LONE
LIZARDS

Stomp! A bearded dragon marches across its territory alone.

Most bearded dragons live alone. Each one has its own area called a territory. They do not like to share space.

If two dragons meet, there can be trouble. The bigger one may push the smaller one away. It may even sit on top of the other. They do this to show who is boss!

Sometimes a smaller dragon waves one arm in a slow circle. This gentle move means, 'I am no threat.' Then it walks away.

When two male bearded dragons fight, they bite, shove, and even roll around like tiny wrestlers!

HEAD BOBBING

Bob, bob! A male bearded dragon pumps its head up and down.

When it is time to mate, males put on a show. A male bobs his head up and down fast. This tells nearby females he is strong.

His throat flap fans out wide. His body may show brighter colors. He struts and stomps to look his very best.

If a female likes the show, she bobs her head slowly. Then the two dragons come together to mate.

A male bearded dragon's beard can turn jet black during his mating display, the darker the beard, the more impressive!

TINY DRAGONS

Crack! A tiny bearded dragon pokes its nose out of an egg.

A mother bearded dragon digs a hole in the sand. She lays up to 30 eggs at once! Then she covers them with dirt.

The eggs sit in the warm ground for about two months. The heat helps them grow. Inside each egg, a tiny dragon takes shape.

Each baby has a tiny tooth on its nose. When it is ready to hatch, it uses this tooth to cut the shell. Out wiggles a brand-new dragon!

A baby bearded dragon is only about three inches long when it hatches!

ON THEIR OWN

A mother bearded dragon can lay eggs two or three times in one season!

Poof! The mother slips away and leaves the eggs behind.

Baby bearded dragons get no help from their parents. Once the mother buries her eggs in a sandy nest, she walks away for good. The babies are completely on their own from the moment they dig out of the ground.

Hatchlings live off egg yolk for the first few days. After that, they must start hunting tiny ants and small bugs all by itself. It also has to watch out for birds, snakes, and bigger lizards that would love an easy snack.

Many babies do not survive the first year. But the ones that do grow up fast, almost one inch each month! They are tough little survivors

TOUGH SURVIVORS

Shhh! A bearded dragon sits still. It blends into the rock.

Bearded dragons have many tricks to stay alive. They can change color! They turn darker to soak up more heat and lighter to cool down.

Their brown and tan skin blends in with rocks and dirt. A predator may walk right past and never see them.

In cold months, bearded dragons slow way down. They hardly eat or move. This deep rest is called **brumation**. It is a lot like hibernation in bears, but the dragon does not fully fall asleep. It wakes up now and then to take a sip of water, then goes right back to resting. This helps them save energy until warmer days return.

PET PALS

FUN FACT!
Pet beardies may close their eyes when stroked on the head. This means they're relaxed!

Click, click! A pet bearded dragon taps its nails on its glass tank.

Many bearded dragons live in homes as pets. If you meet one, tiptoe up to the tank and pause. When you stay calm and quiet, your beardie learns you are safe. If you move too fast, it may freeze like a statue or dash to a hiding spot.

Look for a friendly hello. A slow arm wave is your beardie saying, "I notice you!"

And when it spreads out flat under the lamp, it is warming up. Heat helps its body work right, so it can eat and move.

GLOSSARY

basking
Sitting in the sun to warm up the body

brumation
A deep rest some reptiles take when it is cold

cold-blooded
Having a body that cannot make its own heat

feral
A tame animal that has gone back to living wild

hatchling
A baby animal that has just come out of its egg